HOW ARE THEY BUILT?

ROLLER COASTERS

Lynn M. Stone

Rourke Publishing LLC
Vero Beach, Florida 32964

www.rourkepublishing.com

PHOTO CREDITS:
Cover © Corel; pages 6, 13, 16, 19, 28, 30, 38 ©Armentrout; pages 4, 20, 21, 27 ©Kennywood; pages 11 ©Dynamic Designs; page 23 ©Photo Disc, Inc. pages 9, 31, 32, 35, 41 ©Paramount's Kings Island

EDITORIAL SERVICES:
Pamela Schroeder

ABOUT THE AUTHOR:
Lynn Stone is the author of more than 400 children's books. He is a talented natural history photographer as well. Lynn, a former teacher, travels worldwide to photograph wildlife in its natural habitat.

Library of Congress Cataloging-in-Publication Data

Stone, Lynn M.
   Roller coasters / Lynn M. Stone
      p. cm. — (How are they built?)
   Includes bibliographical references and index.
   ISBN 1-58952-134-X
   1. Roller coasters—Design and construction—Juvenile literature. 2. Roller coasters—Juvenile literature.

GV1860. R64 S86 2001   2001041662
688.7—dc21

Printed In The USA

TABLE OF CONTENTS

Roller coaster rides are thrilling, but safe.

ROLLER COASTERS

Very few people can afford to hitch a rocket ride into outer space. And the military doesn't offer passenger rides in their jets. But no one has to miss a chance for a thrill ride. For a safe and affordable thrill ride, a roller coaster is the answer for most. It's a chance to take 200-foot (61-meter) plunges at 90 miles (144 km) per hour with a few barrel rolls and heart-stopping twists tossed in.

*Watching riders on a looping roller coaster is
enough to make you dizzy.*

Some people, of course, never get past the *looking* stage. They see small coaster cars on narrow tracks zooming around atop towering frameworks of wood or steel. They see the cars in a coaster **train** roar up, down, and around with dizzying speed. They hear the riders' non-stop screaming, especially if they're in a modern theme park. And for some people, that's enough—to watch and listen. There are people who have no interest in scrambling their stomachs and brains on a ride that was *designed* to frighten them.

But roller coaster fans will tell you that being frightened is part of the fun. Most people, sooner or later, put their fears aside and climb aboard. For many, that first roller coaster ride is the start of a long love affair with the scream machines. The whoosh of the wind and the rush of the coaster play tricks with stomachs and brains. But that's part of the fun, too. Cars, elevators, trains, and passenger jets can't match what you feel riding a roller coaster.

At a distance, roller coasters look like the framework of huge railroad trestles. But unlike trestles, roller coasters look like they have been rolled and weaved into shape. Their framework rises and falls in a snakelike way. Both wooden and steel frames support coaster tracks. A complete track route is called a **circuit**.

The Son of Beast *at Paramount's Kings Island is the only looping wooden coaster in the world.*

When you get closer you see that the roller coaster has a boarding and disembarking area. In most modern layouts, you board and disembark from the same place. This is the station where the trains start and finish their runs. Nearby are the **dispatchers**, the ride operators who send the trains out. Depending on the kind of roller coaster, one of the train's cars may have as many as 15 passengers.

As a train rumbles away from the station, it climbs a **lift hill**. A roller coaster depends mostly on **gravity** for its power. But at the start of the ride, a coaster train needs to gain height so gravity can work. Most roller coasters creep up a lift hill with some mechanical help. They use a chain lift system. The chain connects onto a chain-linking device, called a chain dog, under each car. The chain system makes the familiar clacking noise of a roller coaster going up its lift hill.

Ride operators check all passengers are securely fastened in their seats before the ride begins.

At the top the cars are released from the chain. They hurtle down the first—and what is almost always the longest—drop of the run. Most roller coaster drops are sloped at about 50 degrees. If you check a watch at 12:05, note the angle of the small hand, on the 12, and the big hand, on the one. The angle where the bottom of the big hand meets the bottom of the small hand is about 50 degrees. That's a steep fall, and it gives the coaster the forward motion it needs to climb the next hill and finish the rest of the circuit.

The downhill part of a roller coaster ride, after the lift hill **ascent**, may begin 13 or 14 stories up—or more. It offers a great view of the park, but few riders relax enough to enjoy it. No sooner has the train topped the lift hill than it drops like a rock. In fewer than 3 seconds it may accelerate from 12 miles (19 km) per hour to 60 (96 km) per hour. The force of the drop makes you feel light-headed. You have not caught your breath when you find yourself roaring into a nearly circular loop. For brief moments, you may travel upside down. But you hardly have time to adjust. You are through the first loop and into another!

*Riders enjoy the thrill of plunging down
steep hills at high speed.*

The ride lasts about as long as a hit song, a little more than two minutes. You are back at the station, it seems, almost before you left it. You are shaken, but smiling. Like many others who rode with you, you head back into line to ride again.

For all of its breakneck speed and special effects, a roller coaster is safe. It is designed and made to be safe. Safety is built in, from seat belts to track brakes and safety wheels. The only real danger is when a rider does something stupid.

Safety wheels are just one of the wheel types on coaster cars. Road wheels run on top of the rails. They carry the cars. Another set of wheels runs below the rail. These are the under friction wheels, also known as up-stop or underside wheels. Under **friction** wheels keep cars from jumping the rails.

A third wheel type, the guide wheel, or side friction wheel, runs sideways along the side of the rail. The wheel system of coaster cars locks them to the track, but locked-on wheels are not the only safety devices.

The brakes of modern roller coasters are powered **pneumatically**—by air pressure. They are located in the middle of the tracks, but they are controlled at the station. Trim brakes slow or stop trains that sensors show are running too fast. Wet tracks, for example, can increase a train's speed. Computer-operated station brakes slow the trains as they enter a station. Computers on some coasters are used to weigh each train. Trains of unequal weight will run at unequal speeds. Spacing between the cars can then be computer-adjusted to avoid any chance of a crash.

Coasters have improved from their wooden ancestors of more than 100 years ago. They continue to grow higher, faster, and longer. There seems to be no limits on the excitement they create.

*The builders of the first roller coasters would be amazed
at today's high-tech thrill rides.*

HISTORY OF ROLLER COASTERS

The earliest roller coasters zipped down slopes, but they had neither wheels nor tracks. They were the sleds that Russians built for their ice-coated, wooden ramps. Catherine the Great took the idea a step further at the Russian Imperial Summer Palace in the late 1700s. She had sleds fitted with wheels so that downhill coasting could be enjoyed in summer as well as winter.

In the early 1800s, the French built ramps with rollers, something like a factory conveyor belt. Sleds could coast downhill on the ramp rollers. Soon the French put wheels on sleds and grooved the ramps to fit the sleds.

As the rides became more popular, new ideas followed quickly. Before long the sleds were being locked onto tracks for their downhill runs. Similar rides appeared in the United States, which, by the late 1800s, had taken over as the center of roller coaster activity. And in 1884 the first "modern" roller coaster, the *Switchback Railway*, appeared. It was built by LaMarcus A. Thompson at Coney Island in Brooklyn, New York. The *Switchback* had two side-by-side tracks. Passengers climbed to the top of a platform to reach the cars and traveled 600 feet (183 m) downward. They zipped along the Coney Island beach at a top speed of 6 miles (9.6 km) per hour.

Roller coaster cars are locked onto the tracks for safety.

Roller coaster trains consist of several cars attached together.

Thompson's coaster was a booming success. The 5-cents-per-passenger ride paid for itself in three weeks! By 1890 Thompson had built dozens of roller coasters in the United States and Europe. He became known as the "Father of Gravity."

Charles Alcoke improved upon the *Switchback* with his *Serpentine Railway* late in 1884. Alcoke's oval track started and ended in the same place, and his coaster raced along at 12 miles (19 km) per hour. Three years later, in Atlantic City, New Jersey, Thompson introduced the first coaster train by attaching coaster cars together.

John Miller, another American coaster pioneer, was one of the great designer-builders of the early 1900s. He created bigger drops, the first racing type coaster, and a safety **innovation**—side friction wheels.

Side friction wheels improved the safety of roller coasters.

In the 1920s most Americans had good jobs, and people were willing to spend money for fun. At the same time, trolley cars and automobiles were making it easier to get around. Amusement parks sprang up almost overnight, like mushrooms. With the parks came a wave of new roller coasters. By 1929 there may have been as many as 1,500 wooden roller coasters.

But by then the roller coaster's Golden Age was nearly over. America slipped into the Great Depression. With jobs hard to find, people had little to spend at amusement parks. After the Depression, America fought in World War II from 1941-1945. Materials that might have been used to repair roller coasters were used instead in the war effort. By 1948 hundreds of roller coasters had been torn down. There were perhaps 350 left, and some of those, too, would soon be torn down. It was not until the 1950s that the roller coaster began its slow comeback.

Amusement park business has had its ups and downs,
but today they are more popular than ever.

Disneyland opened its popular *Matterhorn Bobsled*, the first modern steel roller coaster, in 1959. The coaster did not start a surge of roller coaster construction right away. But the success of Disneyland convinced others to build theme parks. As theme parks grew in the 1970s, they introduced a new generation of roller coasters to a new generation of Americans. The number of major American coasters rose from fewer than 150 in 1979 to more than 200 in the late 1990s.

With their new popularity, and new technology, coasters have become more and more fantastic in design. The first modern looping roller coaster, the *Corkscrew*, appeared in 1976 at Knotts' Berry Farm in Buena Park, California. The first suspension coaster, *Big Bad Wolf*, opened in 1984 at Busch Gardens, Williamsburg, Virginia. The first stand-up coaster, the *King Cobra*, opened at Kings Island, Kings Mill, Ohio, also in 1984. And designers like John Allen and the Bolliger and Mabillard Company have continued to build state-of-the-art coasters.

WHO BUILDS ROLLER COASTERS?

Roller coaster plans are created by designers and **engineers** at roller coaster manufacturing companies. Roller coasters are built for amusement and theme parks throughout the world.

Today's roller coasters are highly engineered, carefully made structures. Computers are as important to roller coaster design as is a team of engineers. Safety, comfort, and thrills are all part of the designers' final goal. But the planning and building of any roller coaster is a careful process. Designers use knowledge of natural forces, human biology, and technology. Early coaster builders had little understanding of **G forces** and how they affect the human body. Designers today look closely at the G forces their coasters will encounter. Thanks to computers, designers can do that job very nicely.

In addition to natural forces and safety, roller coaster designers have to plan around building sites, budgets, and the riders. Many coasters, made for family enjoyment, are scaled down in height, speed, and excitement. Not everyone who rides a coaster is a thrill seeker.

Designers and engineers create blueprints that show how and where the coaster should be built. The planners may make a model before building the real coaster.

KINDS OF ROLLER COASTERS

Roller coasters are wooden or steel, although some wooden coasters have steel parts. Within these two large groups, roller coasters are split into groups based on their designs. There are more kinds of steel coasters than wooden.

Racers give riders an extra thrill by pitting one coaster against another in a race to the finish!

Classic coasters are wooden—those made during the 1920s or made to look like them. Wooden coasters are usually twisters or out-and-backs. Twisters are loaded with turns, drops, and cross-overs. They are popular with riders who like surprises along the circuit. Out-and-backs are simple designs that follow long, oval routes. Some wooden coasters are racers, which have parallel tracks. Each track has a train. The trains leave the station at the same time in a "race" around the circuit and back to the station.

Suspension coasters are among the newest designs in steel. These coasters have enclosed cars that hang below the track. They swing with each turn in the track. Inverted steel coasters also have cars hanging below the track, but these are open-air cars, like ski lift shuttles. Riders' feet dangle in the air, increasing the sensation of flight. Inverted circuits are looping. Suspended coaster circuits are non-looping.

The King Cobra *was the first stand-up coaster ever built.*

Stand-up coasters are another new steel design. Riders stand through the coaster circuit instead of sitting. Among other kinds of steel coasters are figure eights, trackless, indoor, and looping. Looping coasters travel through loops that carry riders upside down.

Steel coasters make up the majority of coasters. Steel coasters tend to be cheaper than wood. That makes them a favorite among many buyers. Steel is also easier to maintain and design. Because steel tracks can be twisted into loops and corkscrews, designers can use greater imagination in planning the circuits.

Wooden coasters, even new ones, look more creaky and old than their steel cousins. If this is poison for some riders, it's potion for others who love the sound and "feel" of classic coasters.

Steel coasters like the Vortex *take riders through a maze of loops and corkscrews.*

*Footings support the weight of huge
roller coaster superstructures.*

TAMING NATURE

Roller coaster engineers have to know how natural forces affect their machines and the people who ride them. All structures have to deal with gravity—the force pulling down on them. A roller coaster framework, or superstructure, has its own weight. Its trains and passengers add more weight. The superstructure directs its weight downward to concrete **footings**. Footings are supports built largely below ground. The coaster **superstructure** is connected to the footings, which secure it to the ground.

How natural forces affect riders is a challenge for coaster designers. Designers want to use natural forces to increase the thrill of the ride without making it unsafe.

Roller coasters roll mostly without motor power because of certain physical laws concerning gravity and motion. The lift hill, for example, brings the coaster train high so that the force of gravity can yank it down the slope. The train picks up speed, thanks to gravity, as it rushes downhill. The closer to the bottom it goes, the faster it goes. The headlong rush downhill gives the coaster **momentum**—the force of motion. The faster the coaster travels, the greater its momentum.

Momentum sweeps the coaster up the next hill. While it loses momentum climbing, it regains some of it on the next downhill trip. That momentum gives it energy to climb the second hill, and so on. Most coasters gather enough momentum on the first drop to take them through the entire circuit. But as a coaster rolls along, it gradually loses its momentum due to friction and **drag**.

Roller coasters use gravity to propel them around the track.

When two objects rub together, they create friction. Coaster wheels against the track create friction. Drag is resistance to an object's movement through the air. Between them, friction and drag steal the coaster's momentum.

Gravity is of key importance to roller coaster designers and riders. Gravity tugs us down. If we jump, we plop right back to Earth. That is gravity at work. The normal gravity we feel is G 1. Astronauts in space feel weightlessness, or zero gravity. That is a G force of 0. If you travel upward at high speed, the G force increases. For instance, when a roller coaster train rushes uphill, the G force increases. When it races downhill, the G force decreases. For the brain, stomach, ears, and joints, a roller coaster ride is a constant conflict of G forces. Fluids in the inner ear, reacting to changing forces, send mixed messages to the brain. For some people, it's the ideal recipe for dizziness or motion sickness.

Positive G forces make riders feel heavier, while negative G forces leave riders feeling weightless.

Extreme G forces can be unpleasant and unsafe. Most modern roller coasters do not exceed a G force of 3.5 at any time. Even that force makes you feel 3 1/2 times heavier. That is about the same force that astronauts feel on takeoff. At least three coasters outside the United States, however, including the *Mindbender* in Canada, pull up to 6.5 Gs on parts of their rides.

The feeling of weightlessness occurs on some coasters when they briefly take riders into a zero gravity situation. It is the rapid switch from positive G forces to negative that lifts riders from their seats and gives what riders call "air time."

Gravity is the key to any roller coaster design.

BUILDING A ROLLER COASTER

Like other great structures, a roller coaster is built in the virtual world of computers first. A computer can find problems with things such as G forces. It can also plot every drop, swerve, and loop. If the computer finds a problem in the coaster design, it can be fixed before it is built.

With plans in hand, the coaster builders can begin building the coaster on the site. First, bulldozers and other earth-moving machines clear away obstacles along the circuit where the coaster will be built. A roller coaster may be small enough to occupy 3 or 4 acres (1.2 or 1.6 hectares) or big enough to occupy 35 acres (14 ha).

After clearing the way, earth-movers may level the ground. Some coasters, though, are built on naturally rolling ground or land features such as ravines.

The construction crew next prepares footings for the superstructure. Roller coaster footings are concrete reinforced with steel rods and steel frames called **rebar**. A footing is constructed by pouring concrete into a deep hole and adding the appropriate steel. Sometimes footings start well below ground level and rise well above it.

Meanwhile, in the case of a steel coaster, the sections that make up the superstructure are made in a coaster company's plant. Every piece has been made according to the engineer's plans. Almost every coaster has its own unique plan. At the building site, a crane lifts the steel support columns and puts them in place.

*Large roller coasters take months to build
and can cost millions of dollars.*

The size of the columns depends upon the kind of coaster. Typical support columns might be 30 inches (77 cm) in diameter. A 4,000-foot (1,219-m) circuit might require about 155 steel support columns. As sections of framework are put up, workers can add sections of track. The people who attach track have to be sure the track sections fit snugly together before they are **welded**.

Construction of a wood coaster is different. Wood planks are delivered to the construction site, where they are measured and cut to size. The planks are bolted together in sections on the ground. Each section is given a number to match with the plans. As a section is completed, a crane hoists it into position directly over the footings. Steel straps in the footings are bolted to the legs. Sections of the frame are bolted to each other with wood beams called **ties**.

With the completion of each section of superstructure—some tall, others low—track is added. The track route of a wooden coaster is made of boards layered on top of each other. The top layers are wide enough to create an overhang. Safety wheels on the cars will travel under the overhang. The side surface of the track has track steel for the side rolling friction wheels. For safety wheels, track steel is used only where G forces will be negative, or where the car may lift. Track steel is not necessary for safety wheels in dips and valleys, where the wheels have no chance of touching the track.

The framework may require special braces. For example, on tracks where there are forces causing powerful side movements of the train, cables are used. Cables are wire ropes that are attached to support beams at one end and to footings on the other.

Even with the superstructure completed, more remains to do. The chain lift, brake system, train detection devices, block system controls, fences, and lighting systems still have to be added. Finally, cars can be set up on the track and tests can begin. Some coasters take a year to build, but most can be set up in 6 months.

Before people ride the new coaster, the cars are run with **mannequins** or sandbags as "riders." When the ride appears to be working perfectly, engineers and park workers become the first live passengers.

Close watch of the coaster will continue for as long as it is in service. Each day, trained inspectors walk over every foot of the track. And during the winter, when northern coasters close down, the cars are carefully checked in shops.

GREAT NORTH AMERICAN ROLLER COASTERS

WOODEN

Cyclone, Astroland (at Coney Island), Brooklyn, New York. A true classic coaster, the *Cyclone* is as much fun today as it was in 1927, when it was built. Its 60-degree first drop is still one of the world's steepest on a wooden coaster.

Texas Giant, Six Flags over Texas, Arlington, Texas. Built in 1990, the *Texas Giant* is one of the tallest, fastest, and largest wooden coasters—truly Texas-sized. The *Giant* also has one of the greatest drops— 137 feet (41 m).

The Beast, Paramount's Kings Island, Cincinnati, Ohio. With a 7,400-foot (2,276-m) circuit, The Beast is the longest wooden roller coaster in the world. Following the rolling landscape, *The Beast* provides an unusually long ride, nearly 4 thrilling minutes!

LeMonstre, La Ronde, Montreal, Quebec, Canada. *LeMonstre*, built in 1985, is Canada's tallest wooden roller coaster at 131 feet (40 m) and one of the tallest in the world.

Riverside Cyclone, Riverside Park, Agawam, Massachusetts. A small but wild coaster, the *Cyclone* has steep drops and fast, tight turns.

Great White, Wild Wheels Pier, Wildwood, New Jersey. *Great White* is built in large part over the shore of Wildwood beach. Built in 1996, *Great White* has the steepest drop of any wooden coaster.

STEEL

Montu, Busch Gardens, Tampa, Florida. Quick and terrifying with switchbacks and tunnels, *Montu* is one of the best inverted coasters.

Superman: The Escape, Six Flags Magic Mountain, Valencia, California. Built in 1997, this is the world's tallest (415 feet/128 m) roller coaster and one of its fastest (100 mph/162 kph).

Steel Force, Dorney Park, Allentown, Pennsylvania. An exceptional blend of height, speed, and distance, *Steel Force* visits the length of Dorney Park and offers great views of the park's other coasters.

Steel Phantom, Kennywood, West Mifflin, Pennsylvania. This is one of the tallest and fastest looping coasters in the world. Its first terrifying drop is followed by a breathtaking 225-foot (69-m) mountainside drop—and speeds up to nearly 90 miles (144 km) per hour.

Alpengeist, Busch Gardens, Williamsburg, Virginia. Like a chair lift in the Swiss Alps, *Alpengeist* takes riders in chair lift style cars below the tracks—but not at chair-lift speed. *Alpengeist* weaves and loops at coaster speed!

GLOSSARY

ascent (eh SENT) — the climb up

circuit (SUR kit) — the entire track route of a
  roller coaster

dispatcher (dis PACH er) — one who sends roller
  coaster trains from the station

drag (DRAG) — the resistance, or friction, caused by air
  against a moving object

engineer (en jeh NEER) — one who applies science and
  math to the design of various structures

footing (FOOT ing) — an underground support, usually
  made of reinforced concrete, on which columns
  can be set

friction (FRIK shen) — the wearing, or rubbing, of one
  object against another

G force (GEE FORS) — a gravitational force, measured
  in negative or positive terms

gravity (GRAV eh tee) — the force that pulls objects
  toward the ground

innovation (in oh VAY shen) — a new and useful idea
  or design

lift hill (LIFT HIL) — the hill from which a roller coaster train begins its run

mannequins (MAN eh kinz) — life-sized, artificial people

momentum (moh MEN tem) — the energy an object gathers as it accelerates, or increases its speed

pneumatically (noo MAT ik eh lee) — relating to being controlled by air pressure

rebar (REE bar) — a framework of steel bars that is filled with concrete

superstructure (SOO per struk cher) — the above-ground framework of a roller coaster

ties (TYZ) — wooden planks used to connect larger planks in a large structure

train (TRAYN) — two or more linked roller coaster cars

welded (WELD ed) — having had one metal piece melted by extremely high heat onto another

INDEX

Further Reading:

Burgan, Michael. *The World's Wildest Roller Coasters*.
    Capstone Press, 2001
Cook, Nick. *Roller Coasters (or I Had So Much Fun I Almost Puked)*.
    Carolrhoda 11 Books, 1998
Urbanowicz, Steven J. *The Roller Coaster Lover's Companion*.
    Citadel Press, 1997

Websites to Visit:

www.rollercoasterworld.com
www.coasters.net
www.coasterquest.com
www.lifthill.com